VD-STD: The Silent Epidemic

For herpes information call 800–200–8922

Margaret O. Hyde

VD-STD: The Silent Epidemic

SECOND EDITION

McGraw-Hill Book Company

New York   St. Louis   San Francisco   Düsseldorf   Johannesburg
Kuala Lumpur   London   Mexico   Montreal   New Delhi   Panama
Rio de Janeiro   Singapore   Sydney   Toronto

ACKNOWLEDGMENTS

The author gratefully acknowledges the information and
assistance provided by the American Social Health Association
and the Venereal Disease Control Division, Centers for Disease
Control, of the Public Health Service.

Photos on page 41 were provided by the Public Relations Office
Medical Center Hospital Burlington, Vermont

Photos on pages 46, 47, 50 were provided by the VD National Hotline.

1 2 3 4 5 6 7 8 9 B K P B K P 8 7 6 5 4 3 2

53062

ISBN 0-07-031651-1

Library of Congress Cataloging in Publication Data
Hyde, Margaret Oldroyd, 1917–
VD-STD, the silent epidemic.
Rev. ed. of: VD: the silent epidemic. [1973]
Summary: Discusses the types of sexually transmitted
diseases and the means of preventing the spread of these
diseases and their complications.
1. Venereal diseases—Juvenile literature.
[1. Venereal diseases] I. Title. II. Title:
V.D.-S.T.D., the silent epidemic.
RC200.2.H92   1982   616.9'51   81–12330
ISBN 0–07–031651–1

84-15186

To Fred Kroger

Education Specialist, Veneral Disease Control Division,
Centers for Disease Control, Atlanta, Georgia

CONTENTS

1

STD (VD)
IS EVERYONE'S
PROBLEM

"This is the most satisfying experience I have ever had," Jane remarked to a new co-worker as she left her desk at the VD hotline. Jane had just completed a week's work as a volunteer. She applied for training soon after her friend Beth's baby died at the age of two months. Although her friend Beth had not been aware of it, she had a sexually transmitted disease that infected her baby as it traveled down the birth canal.

Jane used to believe that VD was someone else's problem. She had often remarked that people who suffered from VD got what they deserved. Now Jane knows that there are many innocent victims. Now she knows that there are about 20 different kinds of venereal diseases and that most of them can be cured. She knows that VD is everyone's problem.

Traditionally, diseases such as syphilis, gonorrhea, and a few other stigma-laden diseases were called VD. Today there is a trend toward replacing the word "venereal" with the words "sexually transmitted" and toward talking about STD rather than VD. In this way such diseases as genital herpes, trich, and scabies may avoid the old stigma.

Since Jane has become a worker at the VD hotline, she has tried to make more people conscious of the various diseases. Now and then, however, people she approaches don't want to talk about STD or learn anything about prevention. They say STD does not affect them. Nevertheless Jane tries to win their interest.

No neighborhood or segment of society remains untouched by the personal tragedy of these diseases. On one hand, there are those individuals who are infected. Many of these, such as newborn babies, play no part in their victimization. On the other hand, there is the general public whose taxes have become part of the two and a half billion dollars a year needed to care for the medical, surgical, and institutional needs of STD victims.

Unfortunately, no one knows how many people are affected by STD, but it is known that more than 300,000 babies are born with such diseases each year. About 10,000 of these babies die in the first few days of life. About 8000 sustain brain damage resulting in mental retardation, blindness, deafness, and spasticity, and 100,000 babies suffer from a variety of eye and respiratory infections. Many of these infants will require lifelong care in institutions.

Young women are primary victims of STD too. About 100,000 women under the age of 30 suffer permanent damage to their reproductive organs each year and most of these women become sterile. Since female anatomy can disguise symptoms of many sexually transmitted diseases for long periods of time, more women than men are victims of STD-related sterility, arthritis, heart diseases, and other long-term consequences. At least two sexually transmitted diseases may play a role in the development of cervical cancer.

Jane has made a firm commitment to help prevent the spread of STD. You may not want to spend as much time

THIS EPIDEMIC IS GETTING OUT OF HAND

HEAD 'EM OFF AT   *1115* NORTH MacGREGOR

CITY OF HOUSTON HEALTH DEPARTMENT

VD Facts - Call JA 9-5353

A humorous VD poster used in the fight against VD

helping as she does, but you may want to join the fight to make people aware of an epidemic of sexually transmitted diseases that is raging needlessly.

2
THE SILENT EPIDEMIC

Today the STD epidemic appears silent when compared with the much publicized epidemics of polio, plague, and typhoid. Many people know more about the diseases of yesterday than about the sexually transmitted diseases that are so widespread today. Many adults do not want to believe that there is a problem in their own community. They go along with the old cliché that "Nice people don't get VD." But when they become aware of many of the risks and complications that can result from the diseases, they are willing to make education available. When these people discover the extent of the problem, few disagree that something should be done to alter the threat that young people face in the next decade.

Sexually transmitted diseases contribute to a million episodes of pelvic inflammatory diseases annually, according to Dr. Paul J. Weisner and Fred Kroger of the Venereal Disease

Control Division, Centers for Disease Control, in Atlanta, Georgia. They report that about two-tenths of a million women are made infertile each year by STD. Of the estimated more than 20 million people who will be victims of such diseases this year, more than half will be under 25 years of age and almost one-fourth will be victimized before they receive their high school diplomas. Dr. Weisner and Mr. Kroger consider STD the most costly, most common, and most destructive disease problem of the young people in America.

Since it is estimated that one of every eight or nine adolescents is stricken with a sexually transmitted disease of one variety or another, one of the health objectives of the eighties is reducing the spread of these diseases and the complications that come from them through effective education.

Relatively few people are even aware of the existence of a disease known as nongonococcal urethritis (NGU). Actually, this is a group of diseases caused by several kinds of organisms, especially Chlamydia, the kind of bacterium that often gives this group of diseases its name. About three million people are believed to be suffering from this little-known disease at any time. About half the cases of a pneumonialike disease in infants under the age of eight weeks are caused by Chlamydia infections transmitted from their mothers.

Although more is being heard about genital herpes, it is still part of a silent epidemic. According to some estimates, this disease now affects as many as 20 million people, and the problem may be growing at a rate of one-quarter million to two million people each year. Genital herpes has been called "the VD of the eighties," the most common cause of venereal disease. The disease is particularly troublesome because there is no cure at the present time.

Many doctors, health workers, and other people are aware that STD is one of the nation's most challenging health problems.

3

RECOGNIZING
SYMPTOMS AND
TAKING ACTION

Since there are at least 20 diseases that are transmitted sexually, there are many different symptoms. However, there are a few common warning signs that appear in the early stages of many of the diseases. Some more specific details are given in the following chapter, but only a medical specialist can diagnose a sexually transmitted disease correctly and prescribe effective treatment. Some diseases can be identified only by specific tests.

If any of the following symptoms occur, it means that something is wrong that should be checked by a physician. These are:

PAINFUL URINATION: a burning sensation and/or frequent urination are symptoms of some venereal diseases, but they may be symptoms of other diseases, too.

DISCHARGE: a "drip" from the penis that is watery or thick may be a symptom of a venereal disease. Women may have some vaginal discharge between menstrual periods that varies in color and consistency, but in many cases no discharge is present. Irritation and itching may be more reliable warning signs for them.

SKIN CHANGES: blisters, sores, rashes, or warts in the genital area may indicate the presence of sexually transmitted diseases, but they can occur with other diseases, too.

ITCHING: some sexually transmitted diseases cause intense itching.

ABDOMINAL PAIN: lower abdominal pain, with or without fever, may be a symptom of gonorrhea or another venereal disease.

A person with a venereal disease may have one or more of these symptoms or may have none at all. A physical examination by a doctor as well as special laboratory tests are important actions to take if you have some symptoms and think you have been exposed.

People who think they have STD behave in many different ways. Sam saved his shorts in the bottom of his bureau drawer day after day, rather than put them in the family laundry. In this way he could delay the time when his mother would question their strange appearance. He thought the "drip" would soon go away. Instead, his gonorrhea grew stronger and harder to treat.

Mary decided upon self-treatment. Since her father was a doctor, she could consult his medical books. Mary recognized the symptoms of syphilis and knew that penicillin was used in its treatment. Since she had some medicine left from a former illness, Mary took the penicillin that she had for as long as it lasted. During that time, her sore throat and fever lessened, and since these symptoms mimic many other diseases, she could pass her illness off as grippe. Even her father did not guess the true nature of the disease.

Mary's symptoms disappeared, but the syphilis did not. She had not taken the proper amount of penicillin. The spirochetes in her bloodstream caused trouble many years later.

Susan knew that she had been suffering from an STD called herpes before she became pregnant. She reported this to her doctor even though she no longer had any active symptoms, nor had the disease been active for several years. Susan was aware of the fact that the virus could become active again and that it could cause serious damage or death for her baby if it became active at the time of delivery.

The doctor assured Susan that the chances of her baby being infected were very small since he would be watching for the presence of the active virus in his periodic checkups as the time for the birth of her baby drew near. Although some babies are born with herpes even when the mothers have no active signs of the disease, many women who have suffered from this disease deliver healthy babies. The doctor told Susan that he would deliver the baby by Caesarean section if he thought there was a chance of infection as the baby passed through the birth canal.

Susan's case is one example of a person who took important action to prevent a possible tragedy. There is a choice of action for anyone who thinks he or she might have been exposed to a venereal disease. Early diagnosis and treatment are important in the prevention of serious consequences.

If you think you have been exposed and/or have suspicious symptoms you can:

1. Call the VD National Hotline at 1–800–227–8922 toll-free from any place in the United States. If you are in California, call 1–800–982–5883 unless you are within area code 415. In this area, call 327–5301.

The VD National Hotline is an information and referral service that provides live operator coverage seven days a week, 14 hours a day (from 8:30 A.M. to 10:30 P.M. Pacific time). At other times a recorded message gives general VD information and emergency procedures.

This VD hotline can make referrals to over 5000 public

and private local medical facilities that stand ready to provide free or low-cost VD diagnosis or treatment.

2. Discuss your concern and/or symptoms with your own physician.

3. Look in the yellow pages of your telephone directory under CLINICS. Many communities have special clinics for the treatment of STD. Sometimes help is available from a community health center or hospital clinic.

No matter which approach you choose, it is important to seek medical help if you think you might have a sexually transmitted disease. Early treatment can prevent much suffering, many complications, and the spread of disease to others. Even though some sexually transmitted diseases are more serious than others, all require medical attention. Self-diagnosis and/or home remedies can be ineffective and even dangerous for yourself and other people.

4

SEXUALLY
TRANSMITTED
DISEASES:
A WIDE VARIETY

Venereal diseases include a wide variety of ailments that have one thing in common: they are sexually transmitted. Some of the most common and important of them are described in this chapter for easy reference. Others include: chancroid, amebiasis, cytomegalovirus infection (see page 39), giardiasis, granuloma inguinale, group B streptococcal disease, hepatitis B, molluscum contagiosum, shigellosis, and more.

CANDIDIASIS (MONILIASIS, YEAST, OR THRUSH)

Candida albicans is a yeast that normally lives in about 50 percent of healthy people. It is found in the mouth, the intestines, and in the vagina of about 20 percent of nonpregnant women. Sometimes it produces symptoms in the form of a white discharge that has been compared with the consistency of cottage cheese. Itching and a strong odor may be present.

Yeast infection increases at certain times and under

certain circumstances. For example, symptoms are often worse before menstruation. The use of birth control pills, pregnancy, diabetes, chronic infectious diseases, and other conditions tend to lower resistance to ycast infections. Heat and moisture are favored conditions for the growth of this fungus, so some doctors recommend that women who have symptoms avoid wearing pantyhose.

Candidiasis can be spread by sexual contact, and males may develop an inflammation at the tip of the penis from contact with infected women. This inflammation is known as balanitis.

GONORRHEA

Gonorrhea ranks high among the reported communicable diseases in the United States, although unreported sexually transmitted diseases are probably much more common than supposed. A new and easier test for gonorrhea was approved for use in the Spring of 1982. As a result, the number of cases reported annually is expected to increase from the one million cases formerly reported. There may be as many as three million cases reported each year. Although information about the identification of gonorrhea must be reported, information about the patient is confidential.

Screening programs, in which large numbers of people are tested to discover if any persons in the group have the disease, appear to have played a part in preventing the spread of gonorrhea. However, no one can be certain of the true number of cases because of different reporting practices among physicians. It is certain that the number of reported cases among women rose when male patients were encouraged to bring their female partners for medical care. This did not mean that there was an increased number of cases of the disease, but it appeared to be so because more cases were being reported. Actually, this practice reduces the prevalance of gonorrhea because more cases are treated.

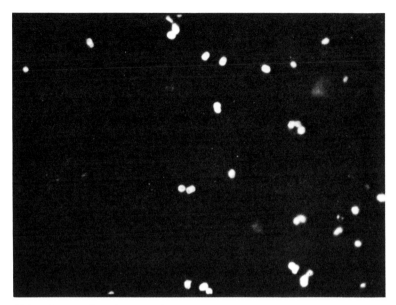

Neisseria gonorrhea, the gonorrhea germ

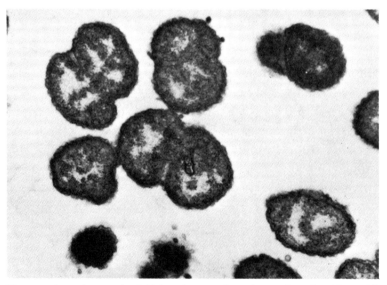

Electron photomicrograph of *Neisseria gonorrheae* (approximately 100,000 X), which causes gonorrhea

The symptoms of gonorrhea are more easily recognized in the male than in the female. Any time within twenty-four hours from the time the bacteria of gonorrhea (*Neisseria gonorrheae*) are introduced into the sexual organs or another area of mucous membrane, symptoms may appear in boys and men. Usually the symptoms begin between the third and the eighth day of infection and consist of pain during urination and the secretion of pus. Both sperm cells and urine pass through the same tube in the male, a passageway known as the urethra.

Some girls and women have symptoms with gonorrhea. For example, they have pain and urinate more frequently than usual, and some have a discharge from the vagina, but in most cases there are no symptoms in the female.

The urine of the female passes through her urethra, but this is separate from her reproductive system. Infection in the vagina of the female may destroy its delicate linings, along with the linings of other parts of the reproductive system. Untreated gonorrhea may make it impossible for a girl to bear a child in future years.

The early symptoms of gonorrhea disappear without treatment. Even though the symptoms go away, the disease is not cured. It can almost always be cured if treated in its early stages. But men as well as women may have sex organs infected by gonorrhea germs that migrate to other areas of the body as the disease progresses. This may make it necessary for surgical removal of damaged organs.

Possible complications of untreated gonorrhea, in addition to damage to sex organs and sterility, include infections that can cause damage to heart tissue, joints, and other tissue.

Penicillin or other antibiotics can cure gonorrhea but they cannot repair organs that are damaged. While antibiotics other than penicillin usually cure new and more serious strains of gonorrhea, there is danger that these strains will eventually become resistant to the other antibiotics.

HERPES PROGENITALIS (GENITAL HERPES or HERPES SIMPLEX II)

Genital herpes is a major health problem in the United States since about 20 million people are affected, and estimates of new cases per year range from one-quarter million to two million.

The virus that causes genital herpes is closely related to the one that causes fever blisters and cold sores. These, too, are called herpes, for the microorganism that causes them is *Herpes Simplex I*. Together, the number of victims ranges from 50 to 150 million.

An estimated 30 percent of sexually active adults in the United States have been exposed to genital herpes, but not all who are exposed contract the disease. For those who do, symptoms can include painful, itching sores or blisters that appear on or around the genitals from two to 20 days after infection. A burning sensation during urination is another symptom. Fever and other flulike symptoms may develop too.

The sores heal in about two or three weeks, but some viruses remain in the body in a dormant state for one's lifetime. Some people never experience the painful, itching sores after the initial infection, while others have recurrences that vary from frequent to rare. Usually recurrences are less severe than the initial infection. Occasional flare-ups may be related to poor general health, stress, various foods, or other conditions. The reasons for recurrences are not fully understood.

Genital herpes is highly contagious while the blisters persist. The virus can be transmitted to another person and/or to a new location on the body by contact. Keeping the area of the sores dry and clean can help to prevent transfer to another part of the body.

Infection can be spread even when there are scabs on the sores so it is important that the victim avoid contact until the sores are completely healed. Fingers and eyes are especially vulnerable to herpes infection. When eyes become infected, blindness can result. In fact, herpes is a leading cause of blindness among young adults, but treatment with new compounds that have been developed can greatly reduce the chance of permanent problems. Washing hands after touching sores can help to prevent the spread of herpes.

At present no cure is available for genital herpes, but researchers are working with some promising new drugs. Through the years, herpes victims have tried to cure the disease with a long list of supposed remedies ranging from cactus sap to volcanic ash applied to the sores. On March 30, 1982, the Food and Drug Administration announced approval of topical acyclovir, the first drug to "help manage" genital herpes. This drug is not a cure, but it does shorten some of the symptoms.

A program service of the American Social Health Association offers a special kind of help for herpes victims who are experiencing difficulties in coping with the disease. If you are interested in becoming a member of the program, which is known as HELP, you can obtain further information about it by writing to HELP/ASHA, 260 Sheridan Avenue, Palo Alto, California 94306.

A quarterly journal called *The Helper* is published by the American Social Health Association and is available to members of HELP. This journal includes reports on prevention, new research on medication, and actions that can be taken by all who want to support the fight against herpes.

HELP provides access to local support groups and a private HELPLINE for personal concerns and assistance in coping.

Herpes is not a new disease. There have been records of it for at least two thousand years. What is new is the recognition of the size and severity of the current epidemic of genital herpes and its potential relationship to cervical cancer. Action to prevent its spread and possible complications is both recent and important.

Although there is still no proven cause-and-effect relationship between herpes and cervical cancer, scientists report that women who suffer from genital herpes are five to eight times as likely to develop cervical cancer as those who do not. It has been proven that the herpes virus is a significant risk factor in the transformation of normal cells into defective ones.

The Pap test, which is performed routinely by many doctors who do annual pelvic examinations for their patients, reveals cervical abnormalities and cell changes before cancer develops. Women who have a history of genital herpes are advised to have a Pap test every six months. Simple treatment can prevent abnormal cells from developing into cancer when such changes are detected early.

Complications of herpes and pregnancy are discussed in a later chapter of this book.

LYMPHOGRANULOMA VENEREUM

Lymphogranuloma venereum is a common tropical venereal disease that is caused by an organism related to those causing such diseases as parrot fever. The causative organism is also a member of the Chlamydia family. (See NGU.) The germ is similar in some ways to a virus and in other ways to a bacteria. No matter how one classes the cause, the disease can be very destructive if not properly treated.

Sometime between one and 12 but usually within 21 days after exposure to the germ, a small ulcer appears on the sex organs. It is so small that women sometimes do not notice its presence. In some cases there is a burning pain when an infected person urinates. Soon after the sore disappears, the lymph nodes in the groin may swell and become painful, and as the disease continues, they become more inflamed, and pus may drain through passageways that extend from the lymph nodes.

If lymphogranuloma venereum is not treated, the skin sores and the inflammation will probably gradually disappear, but internal damage may include scarring and closing around the rectum and anus in women. Some cases become complicated by cancerous changes.

Treatment for LGV, as it is sometimes called, is usually with sulfa drugs or drugs from the tetracycline group. Penicillin is not used here. Once more, as with other venereal diseases, early treatment greatly improves the chance for a complete cure.

NONGONOCOCCAL URETHRITIS (NGU)

NGU includes all urethritis infections not caused by the bacteria that cause gonorrhea. There are several kinds of NGU, but the most common appears to be caused by an organism known as Chlamydia, for which the disease is sometimes named. The symptoms are more noticeable in men than in women but both usually have a discharge about three weeks after infection. This is thin at first, but it becomes thick, white, and creamy and the symptom is often mistaken for gonorrhea. In some cases, there is no discharge in men. Painful urination may be a symptom too. A physician can make tests to determine the identity of the disease, a procedure that often begins with tests to eliminate the possibility of gonorrhea.

Possible complications of NGU include sterility in both men and women. In men, the sperm ducts can become inflamed and blocked. In women, pelvic inflammatory disease (PID) can result, causing inflammation and blocking in the fallopian tubes that carry the ova to the uterus.

Although many people are not even aware that there is a group of sexually transmitted diseases called nongonococcal urethritis, this group of diseases is becoming increasingly common. Some doctors believe that they will be included in the list of reportable diseases when testing is less expensive and difficult. There are probably more than three million cases of NGU in the United States each year. Routine testing is uncommon, but cases that are recognized can easily be treated with antibiotics. NGU is sometimes considered a potential cause of a sterility epidemic.

PEDICULOSIS PUBIS (CRABS or LICE)

Pubic lice are oval, grayish insects that become reddish brown when engorged with blood. They attach themselves to pubic hairs and cause itching. They are usually spread by close bodily contact but they can be spread by contaminated clothing or bedding.

Itching is characteristic. Sometimes small blood spots are distinguishable on underwear and lice may be seen moving on the skin.

Pubic lice can be identified with a magnifying glass. Medicated shampoos, lotions, and ointments are available for treatment. All contacts should be treated and clothing and bedding must be kept especially clean during treatment.

SCABIES

Scabies is caused by a mite that can live on many parts of the body, but the most common sites are finger webs, wrists, elbows, underarms, ankles, and genitals. Although it can be transmitted by any close body contact with an infected area, infested bedding, or infested clothing, scabies is included with other sexually transmitted diseases because sexual contact is a common way for it to spread. Mites burrow under the skin, causing small red areas that itch at night for about four to six weeks after infection.

The disease can be diagnosed by microscopic indentification of the scabies mites or by recognition of the type of burrow that they make. Complications include impetigo and pustular eczema, but medicated creams can be applied to infected areas after baths to treat the condition. Family members and others in close contact with a person who has scabies should be aware of the possibility that the mite may have spread to them.

SYPHILIS

Syphilis was once commonly known as pox, syph, siff, bad blood, Old Joe, haircut, and lues. No matter what it is called, this disease can cause unbelievable misery, such as insanity and paralysis, if not cured by treatment in the early stages.

Biblical scholars have found references to diseases believed to be syphilis and gonorrhea in the books of Genesis and Leviticus, and it is believed that history itself may have been changed at times because of syphilis. The cruelty of Henry VIII in the later years of his reign may have been due to syphilitic insanity. Many other individuals who were prominent in the pages of history were thought to be its victims along with numerous less known people.

Syphilis ranks third (exceeded only by gonorrhea and chickenpox) among the reported communicable diseases in the United States. This is sad indeed, since syphilis is preventable and curable.

One of the first signs of syphilis is a hard painless sore that usually appears in the area of the sex organs, but it might possibly break out anywhere on the body. Sometimes no sore appears at all, in which case there is no early warning of the disease. This sore is called a chancre (pronounced "shanker"). It is not usually filled with pus or tender to touch, but feels somewhat rubbery, or like a button under the skin.

Since the sore may appear anytime between ten and 90 days after exposure, many people do not connect the chancre with sexual activity that happened long before. The chancre is more obvious in the male, since it usually appears on the penis. A girl may not notice a sore that appears near her vagina, the canal from her uterus, or womb. Occasionally a chancre occurs in the mouth, but only if this is where the contact has taken place. If a sore does appear, it goes away, healing in a period of about ten days to three weeks.

Anytime from the appearance of the chancre until about three or four weeks from its disappearance, other symptoms may begin. A rash may appear on some parts of the body, but

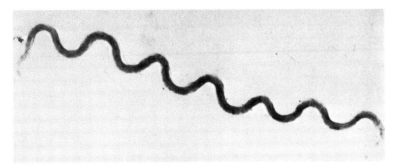

Treponema pallidum, the bacterium that causes syphilis

it will not itch. The rash is the most common symptom of syphilis; but there are many cases in which the chancre or the rash, or both, are very inconspicuous and may not be noticed by the infected person. Patches of hair may fall out from the head, and a mild fever, sore throat, headache, and similar common symptoms may appear. Many of the symptoms are like those of a cold and may not be recognized as part of the pattern of syphilis. At this stage, many people who have been infected have no idea that they really have a venereal disease.

For the uninformed, or for those who do not go for medical care because of feelings of guilt, embarrassment, or fear, syphilis can become a very serious disease. The symptoms described above disappear in time, but the disease may not have been conquered by the body's defense system. The "silent" syphilis is not always the end, for at this point the spirochetes may be multiplying in the bloodstream, where they begin their attack on various organs, such as the heart, the spinal cord, and the brain.

Sometimes syphilis does not appear again after the rash has gone. If the disease gives no symptoms after four or more years have passed, the patient is said to have late latent syphilis. The word "latent" means present but not visible. Although the disease is potentially able to achieve an active stage, it lies dormant. Even though a blood test may be positive, showing that this person is still infected with syphilis, the disease will not spread at this stage unless the patient is a woman and becomes pregnant. Then it may pass to her unborn child if she bears one in less than five years after her infection. Congenital syphilis is the most common serious problem caused by syphilis today.

At the stage where there are no outward signs, the person with syphilis may feel entirely well. While syphilis may be conquered by some people's defense systems and die out, it lingers in other people and breaks out as much as 20 years later. (Sometimes people who have heart attacks do not realize that they are caused by syphilis.) The central nervous system may be infected and the destruction of nerve centers may eventually result in what is known as syphilitic insanity. Severe crippling or paralysis or blindness may occur.

Since syphilis can be cured far more easily than many other diseases, it is especially sad that people still suffer and die from this disease. From a medical point of view, syphilis is relatively easy and inexpensive to diagnose and treat.

TRICHOMONIASIS

Trichomoniasis is a disease that is usually transmitted by sexual contact. The microscopic, one-celled animal that causes it is a parasite known as a protozoan. It can live on damp towels and clothing for a few hours so it is possible for it to spread through contact with another person's towel or clothing though this is not likely.

Men may not develop any symptoms after contact, but women victims usually have a frothy yellow-green discharge with a strong odor that causes irritation and itching. The discharge appears from four to 28 days after infection.

Trichomoniasis is identified through a culture, and drug treatment is available for those who have the disease. Medication is administered differently for pregnant women than for others, so it is important for a woman who is pregnant to tell the physician who is treating her about the pregnancy if it is not obvious.

About a million people are infected with trichomoniasis each year. There are indications that repeated trichomoniasis may predispose a woman to cervical cancer.

VENEREAL WARTS

Venereal warts, like other warts, are caused by a virus. They may be grayish, white, pink, or slightly yellow in color, but no matter what the color, they can be passed from one person to another through sexual contact. The warts usually appear as raised cauliflowerlike growths within or on the area of the genitals and anus. They may develop in the warm, moist environment of the throat too.

These warts are known medically as papillomas condyloma, or just condyloma. Although symptoms of this disease may appear about two weeks after contact, they may not be noticeable until a much longer period has passed. Sometimes people do not notice them until eight months after they have been infected, but these victims may infect others even when the warts are in the incubation stage.

The warts may be recognized by just looking at them, although they may be confused with other diseases. In fact, a growth that is suspected to be cancer may be venereal warts and vice versa. Medical tests can identify venereal warts so that they can be treated with proper medication.

The most common medication is the mild acid podophillyn, but this may cause severe complications for certain people and should be used only under the advice of a doctor. Sometimes, venereal warts are removed surgically, or by the use of liquid nitrogen, or through a treatment known as electrodesiccation. Some treatments cause scarring, but lack of treatment can be worse. For most people, genital warts are more of a cosmetic than a health problem.

5
PREVENTING
THE SPREAD
OF STD

This book is not concerned with the right and wrong of sexual activity. It *is* concerned with ways to recognize, prevent, and cure sexually transmitted diseases. And it is concerned with changing attitudes so that people will seek treatment if they think they might have been exposed to such a disease and with attitudes that will encourage research to improve conditions for victims, who range in age from newborns to the elderly.

How does one know about exposure? Is sexual contact the only way such diseases are spread?

Actually, there are many ways to get a sexually transmitted disease, but the most likely way is through sexual contact. It is not entirely impossible to get syphilis from a toilet seat or a doorknob, but conditions would have to be *very* unusual. In fact, they would have to be so unusual that getting VD from a toilet seat is a standing joke. The organisms that cause most STDs need warm, moist, dark places in which to grow.

Suppose a person suffering from a venereal disease left some infectious organisms in a bathroom immediately before you touched the place where they were deposited. And suppose you touched the place in an area of your body where the skin was broken or where mucous membranes were exposed.

Most of the organisms that cause an STD must find their way into the body through mucous membranes. Since mucous membranes are found in the birth canal (vagina), the urethra, through which urine passes, the rectum, the eyelids, and the throat, you can see that such exposure is unlikely. In some diseases, such as syphilis, germs can enter through the skin, especially in an area where there is a cut. There is *very* little chance that you can contract a venereal disease without person-to-person contact, but that contact is not always sexual in nature.

Theoretically, a dentist could get syphilis when working on the mouth of a person who had a chancre there. The syphilis organisms could enter the body through a cut in the dentist's skin if he came in contact with the infection in the patient's mouth, but such a situation is very unlikely.

Sometimes infections are spread by careless cleansing from the rectum toward the vagina in females and by certain types of sexual activity. All types of STDs can be spread this way.

As mentioned earlier, genital herpes can be spread by direct contact with sores when the disease is in the active state. Nearly 100 percent of all cases of herpes are spread by direct contact from one person to another. Since the virus that causes herpes is smaller than the latex molecules of a condom, it is not impossible for it to pass through. However, this has never been demonstrated in a laboratory. Recent studies indicate that herpes viruses can survive outside the body for as long as 72 hours on inanimate objects such as towels and bed linen. The virus can be destroyed by washing any potentially contaminated object with detergent, hot water, and bleach.

Anyone who has herpes sores, even those that have scabs on them, should avoid contact of these sores with another person. Washing hands helps to prevent the spread to various parts of the victim's own body, but it does not prevent its spread in sexual contact with another person.

People who have herpes spread the disease at times when there is an initial infection, and when there is a recurrence. Sometimes the virus can be transmitted just before a recurrence, a state that people may learn to recognize by an itch, a tingling, an insistent ache, a feeling of pressure, or a throb that occurs within several hours to several days before a recurrence. Just before the recurrence, viruses are active beneath the surface of the skin and the disease may be spread by contact then.

There is nothing complicated about preventing the spread of herpes by avoiding contact when the disease is clearly present. However, it is commonly spread when neither person is aware that there is disease present with which to come in contact.

While most organisms that cause STD die very quickly when not harbored by the human body, as mentioned earlier, the parasite that causes trichomoniasis can survive for a few hours on damp towels, clothing, and bedding. Scabies, lice, and some of the other causative agents can be spread in such ways, but this is unusual.

One of the most important ways of preventing the spread of STD is to stop the chain of infection. This is mainly the responsibility of the people who become aware of the fact that they have contracted a sexually transmitted disease. They can protect the health of sex partners by informing them of the problem and advising them to seek immediate medical care. Health or social workers can help victims to make the process of informing others less difficult. *84-15/85*

Although most people who contract a sexually trans-

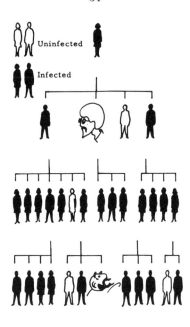

This diagram shows how Betty infected three men, who then infected thirteen other people, who in turn infected ten others.

mitted disease are themselves engaged in sexual relations with just one partner, there are exceptional cases. For example, in one clinic, twelve boys and girls, ranging in age from thirteen to nineteen, are sitting in the hallway of a clinic. They are trying to be casual, acting as if they really do not care much about being there, pretending that they are not frightened, but they really are. They have been called in for a checkup because they have had sexual contact with someone who has syphilis. If they are suffering from the beginning stages of the disease, they can be easily treated and cured. As a result, the people in this group will not begin a new chain of infection.

Chains of infection may sometimes be broken by bringing in the people involved for examination and treatment, as just described. This method, known as the contact inter-view, has been a tool in syphilis-control programs for more than thirty years. It is one method that attempts to cope with the problem, but the difficulties of collecting data on all the contacts of a patient, following the leads, and then bringing the contacts to doctors for testing and treatment are obvious.

One of the main goals of a prevention program is the identification of people who have the disease or who have been exposed to it. Most health departments treat exposed persons, even if they show no signs of the disease, just in case it might be developing. Certainly one of the most effective ways of controlling venereal disease is to prevent new cases from occurring.

Prompt and intensive follow-up by persons skilled in contact interviewing has averted untold numbers of further infections, according to the American Social Health Associa-tion. This organization reports a typical example of how STD spreads. One fourteen-year-old boy was the source of an outbreak of infectious syphilis that eventually involved sixty-six other students in a Texas high school. Forty-one boys and girls needed treatment, and twenty-five others in the group were found to be disease-free.

Here are some other examples of good results in disease prevention by means of contact interviews and a web of activity in which Public Health workers stopped further spreading of venereal disease.

One thirteen-year-old girl in California named thirty-five contacts. She had spread gonorrhea to twenty young boys and men whose ages ranged from twelve to twenty years.

In a case in Mississippi, thirteen people with syphilis were traced to one individual, and the chain was finally found to include ninety contacts. Of these, there were twenty known cases of syphilis. The outbreak was mainly among men, who spread it by sexual contacts with male partners. In this whole case study, only three females were involved.

The World Health Organization reports the case of a

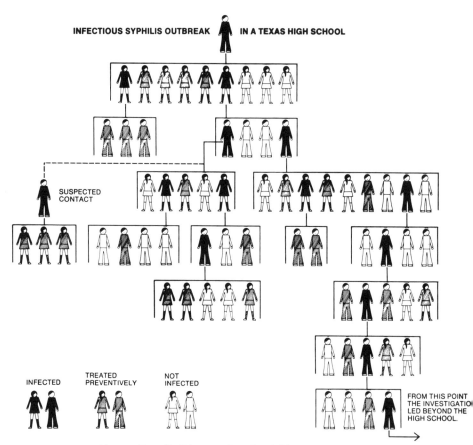

INFECTIOUS SYPHILIS OUTBREAK **IN A TEXAS HIGH SCHOOL**

SUSPECTED CONTACT

INFECTED

TREATED PREVENTIVELY

NOT INFECTED

FROM THIS POINT THE INVESTIGATIO LED BEYOND THE HIGH SCHOOL.

How a Deadly Disease Involved 66 teenagers!

The American Social Health Association reports that a 14-year-old boy was the source of an outbreak of infectious syphilis which eventually involved 66 other students in a Texas high school. Here, an artist illustrates the chain of infection. Forty-one boys and girls were treated, while 25 others in the chain were found to be disease-free. ASHA said prompt and intensive follow-up by "VD detectives" had averted "untold numbers of further infections." The association has conducted continuing campaigns against VD for more than half a century.

fourteen-year-old girl in the United States whose syphilis treatment led to the discovery of early syphilis in seventeen individuals whose average age was only 10.1 years.

Efforts to *control* the silent epidemic of sexually transmitted diseases through contact tracing have been very successful in controlling syphilis but have not been used widely enough to control gonorrhea or other STDs.

Many private physicians fail to report their cases to Public Health officers. The amount of confidence patients have in their doctors may determine how willing they are to tell of their sexual contacts. Doctors have mixed feelings about reporting cases, partly because they want to protect their patients' privacy. While reporting a friend may be the kindest thing to do, so that the friend can obtain early treatment, this is not easy. The approach of the interviewer in establishing trust can play a large part in whether or not further cases of disease can be prevented by successful treatment of people exposed to the original patient.

If all contacts could be found in every chain of infection and treated until they were cured, it would theoretically be possible to eliminate STD. There would be no uncured infectious people to pass the diseases along. But this is an impossible dream. The programs of contact tracing, no matter how dedicated and extensive, can only lower the rate or slow the spread of these diseases in the United States and other countries where privacy is respected.

6

BABIES
AND STD

One of the rewards in working actively in the prevention efforts and in supporting research for cures of sexually transmitted diseases is the realization that you are helping to save innocent babies from the consequences of these diseases.

The tragedy of the babies who become victims of STD before, during, or after birth creates a profound challenge to help spread awareness of the silent epidemic. Perhaps the real tragedy is the needlessness of most infant venereal diseases.

No one knows how many young people would be more careful to avoid sexual contact with an infected person if they were aware of the risk of involuntary sterilization or maternally imparted venereal diseases. Nor does anyone know how many more pregnant women would share information about their own experiences with STD with their doctors if they were aware of the risk to their babies.

Even the people who feel that VD or STD is someone

else's problem usually join the fight against these diseases when they learn that awareness and treatment can prevent tragedies for infants.

Here are the consequences of some of the venereal diseases in infants that could be prevented by awareness, treatment, or further research:

CMV (CYTOMEGALOVIRUS)
CMV is considered the most common viral cause of nerve impairment in babies. It cripples and retards more infants than German measles (*rubella*). No one knows how the virus is transmitted from mother to infant. It is believed that it may come from external contact with the mother's body or it may be transmitted through the placenta, the passageway through which nourishment reaches the unborn baby.

Medical scientists estimate that one of every thousand babies born each year in the United States is seriously retarded or otherwise neurologically impaired as a result of infection with CMV. Other estimates indicate that 25 percent of all serious infant retardation and 20 percent of all infant cerebral palsy is caused by congenital cytomegalovirus.

Although there is still some mystery about how CMV is spread in adults, there is growing evidence that it is transmitted mainly by direct contact and often by sexual contact. The disease may be misdiagnosed as mononucleosis in adults, but it usually does not cause any symptoms in them, so most victims do not know they have it. CMV is considered one of the least understood of the many diseases that are grouped together as STD.

GENITAL HERPES
Genital herpes, when in its active stage, poses a serious threat to babies at the time of delivery because of the high chance of infection as the baby travels down the birth canal. Delivery by Caesarean section eliminates the exposure of the baby to the virus if the disease is active in the mother, and prevents

People are more concerned about STD when they realize that STD may make the

infection in the newborn. Estimates of the number of babies who die as a result of their herpes infection varies from 40 to 80 percent, and even those infected babies who survive may have serious brain damage resulting in mental retardation, blindness, and deafness. Many of these defects are so severe that the sufferers require lifelong institutionalization.

Various drugs are being studied for their promise in improving the prospects of those babies who survive with herpes virus. Researchers at the University of California at Los Angeles found that treatment must begin immediately even in infants with a few insignificant-looking blisters.

GONORRHEA

In most cases a delivery-room nurse treats the eyes of all newborn babies with an antibiotic that protects them from gonorrhea. The treatment is given to all babies, even if there is no question of gonorrhea.

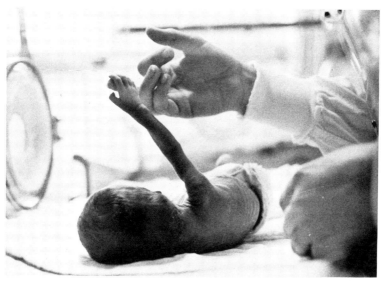

difference between a healthy and a sick baby.

Suppose a mother decides to bear her baby without the help of a doctor. She has exercised in preparation of the great event. She has been very careful of her diet and her general health and has learned how to relax her muscles. And she has prepared for the birth of her child in many other ways.

Friends help in the delivery of the child. Now the baby is safely out of the birth canal, or vagina, and has started to breathe. Soon he will be drinking milk from the mother's breasts. The natural experience seems a joy for all.

This mother and her friends are pollution fighters who have given up material comforts to live in harmony with nature. They are fighting pollution of all sorts with the exception of one. Venereal disease has been called "love pollution," and in the case mentioned above, the baby was pushed and pulled into its new world through a passageway polluted with gonorrhea. His eyes make a suitable home for the fragile germs, and they grow there and blind the child.

NGU (NONGONOCOCCAL URETHRITIS)

Chlamydial organisms, which are responsbile for most cases of NGU, are considered to be the most common cause of a pneumonialike disease in infants under the age of eight weeks. Babies acquire the bacteria from their mothers at delivery. In addition to causing the respiratory disease, Chlamydia creates severe eye infections that can lead to vision impairment if not treated. Pregnant women and children are treated with erythromycin rather than the tetracycline used for most cases of NGU, since the latter can cause discoloration in developing teeth.

SYPHILIS

An untreated mother can pass syphilis to her unborn child, even though her infection began years before her pregnancy. An untreated person is infectious to others for about two years. In the case of pregnancy, the period can be longer.

When babies are born with syphilis, the disease is called congenital. To those who know what this can mean for a young child, the words "congenital syphilis" are ugly indeed. This is especially true since congenital syphilis need not happen.

Suppose a case of syphilis is detected in a woman through a blood test made early in pregnancy. The treatment cures the mother and the baby is safe since the spirochete, *Treponema pallidum,* which causes the disease, does not make its way across the placenta or damage it or the unborn child in the first sixteen weeks. But suppose the disease is not found early in pregnancy. If the syphilis is not treated in the first few months of pregnancy, the fetus may be aborted or the baby may be stillborn. If the baby is born alive, the disease may cause irreparable damage to him or her.

Babies who suffer from congenital syphilis often show signs of injury to teeth and bone tissue. Arms and legs may be shortened, and the skull, face, and teeth may be distorted. The whole face may seem to be pushed in, a condition known as "saddle nose." There may be brain damage resulting in severe mental retardation. Some babies who are born with syphilis are blind because the infection has damaged their eyes before birth.

Treatment of congenital syphilis can make the child noninfectious and prevent further damage from infection, but it cannot repair all that took place during the time the baby was forming.

VENEREAL WARTS

Pregnancy fosters the growth of venereal warts in women who may have contracted the virus even before they became pregnant. Infants can become infected when traveling through the birth canal. Such infection can cause a variety of problems for babies, including warts on the larynx. In certain cases, doctors recommend Caesarean section so that babies do not come in contact with venereal warts.

The tragedies of those born with STD make many young people want to help to make the public aware of the facts about them. The present epidemic will no longer be a silent one if enough of the young people of today accept the challenge to conquer STD by changing attitudes and promoting education so that those who think they might be infected seek early treatment.

7

THE CHALLENGE
OF THE EIGHTIES:
THE ELIMINATION
OF STD

What can you do to help eliminate the tragedies of sexually transmitted diseases and their complications?

One important step in helping to conquer STD is the changing of attitudes and behavior through education. You can encourage your friends to read about these diseases and support programs that promote awareness of the silent epidemic. Write the American Social Health Association, 260 Sheridan Avenue, Palo Alto, California 94306 for information about community activities.

Perhaps you belong to a group who would be interested in developing a community awareness program that provides spot television messages or other media events. Some local public health clinics help to coordinate VD educational programs.

Is there a VD hotline or any hotline that uses volunteers in your community? Many hospitals and clinics train volunteer workers for local hotlines.

Picture a pretty eighteen-year-old girl with long blond hair seated at a desk in a small office with a group of volunteers. A telephone rings. She picks it up and hears a girl at the other end of the line whisper, "How can I tell if I have VD?" The volunteer in the office inquires about her symptoms and tells the caller whether or not she thinks she should visit a clinic or a private physician.

The caller is afraid that her own doctor will tell her parents, so she is referred to a Public Health Clinic near her home.

The phone rings again. A young boy is worried about some symptoms that sound like those of syphilis. The hotline worker cannot diagnose a disease, but she strongly urges this boy to go to his local clinic at once.

No matter what the caller asks, hotline workers are trained to respond in nonjudgmental fashion with advice to seek proper clinical diagnosis. In addition to encouraging early detection and treatment, they play a part in relieving callers' anxieties.

The workers can help sort fact from fiction for those who believe some of the common myths about venereal disease. For example, a caller who believes that once a person has had a certain STD it is impossible to contract it again learns that such is not the case. Another caller who believes that syphilis is inherited learns that it is not, although babies can contract the disease before they are born. Still another caller insists that she is right about getting VD only from someone of the opposite sex. The hotline worker explains that this is a myth.

Then there is the boy who believes gonorrhea can be "caught by lifting heavy things" and is assured that this is not the case. And there is the man who calls to make certain that his gonorrhea has been cured because the drip has stopped. He is advised that the organisms may still be present in his body, and may be traveling through it, damaging tissues even though no symptoms are present. He is encouraged to seek medical treatment so that he can really be cured.

Hotline volunteers receive 15 hours of intensive training prior to working on the lines.

The calls to VD hotlines range from trivial to very serious. Callers may be curious or they may be desperately in need of help. You can see why Jane, the volunteer mentioned on page nine, described her hotline work as the most satisfying experience she has ever had. Some workers say that it is exciting to know that they are helping to prevent diseases that can have such tragic consequences for people, especially for women and for babies.

The stereotype of a VD victim as a young, non-white, inner-city resident does not emerge from VD Hotline data. Here are some facts gleaned from 100,000 Hotline calls as reported by the American Social Health Association in 1982:

1. Sixty percent of the callers are men; forty percent are women.

2. The mean age is 26.5 years.

3. Only 18 percent are less than 20 years old; 30 percent are over 30 years old.

VD National Hotline averages 250 calls per day.

4. Eighty-three percent are white.
5. Eighty-eight percent are heterosexual.
6. Twenty-six percent are married.
7. Almost 20 percent earn more than $25,000 a year.

The first national VD hotline began with an idea of a teenager, Joe Forish, and a Catholic priest, Father Francis X. Schmidt of Philadelphia in 1971. Known as OPERATION VENUS, this hotline was established as a youth-to-youth program that gives information, referral, advice, and transportation to STD victims and people who think they might have STD. The program grew to become a national hotline that served people anywhere in the United States. OPERATION VENUS now operates as a local service only for the Philadelphia area.

A new toll-free national hotline began operations in October 1979 as a program service of the American Social

Health Association, supported in part by grants from the Center for Disease Control in Atlanta, Georgia, and the Santa Clara United Way. This hotline processes over 100,000 phone calls per year and is staffed by volunteers ranging in age from fourteen to seventy-six years.

Anyone who is concerned about symptoms that might mean that he or she has an STD can call the hotline free of charge from anywhere in the United States. The number of the VD NATIONAL HOTLINE is 800–227–8922. In California one calls 800–982–5883.

If you live in the Palo Alto area of California, you may want to answer the call for volunteers who are needed to answer the phones of this information and referral hotline. These workers are given a complete training program in exchange for as little as four hours a week of their time. Some workers arrange to receive high school and college academic credits.

Volunteers are needed on many local hotlines where training is a part of the program. If you are interested in helping to fight STD by working on a hotline, explore the possibilities by contacting your local hospital, clinic, or other community services in your area.

In addition to working on hotlines or promoting VD awareness through media and special events, such as VD Awareness Weeks, anyone interested in helping to stamp out VD can write to his/her Congressmen, asking for additional funding for research. The actual expenditure for research for the prevention and treatment of STD is far below the recommended level of recent study groups concerned with progress in this area. This may be due partly to the attitudes of many people who do not realize that VD, or STD, is everyone's problem.

Just controlling the venereal disease epidemic is a big job. It means more money for research and more help from parents, teachers, organized groups, and especially from young people.

SOME HELP CHAPTERS FOR HERPES VICTIMS

CALIFORNIA

Los Angeles HELP
Box 2881, Culver City, CA 90230

Inland Empire HELP (Los Angeles suburbs)
P.O. Box 4014, Ontario, CA 91761

Long Beach HELP
P.O. Box 5714, Long Beach, CA 90805

Orange County HELP
P.O. Box 125, Yorba Linda, CA 92686

San Diego HELP
P.O. Box 3714, San Diego, CA 92103
(714) 273-6296

Santa Barbara HELP, Freedom Community Clinic
806 Santa Barbara Street, Santa Barbara, CA 93101

Counseling herpes victims on prevention of transmission is an important element of HELP's program.

San Francisco HELP
P.O. Box 6621, San Francisco, CA 94101
(415) 863-9580 (evenings)

San Francisco/East Bay HELP
Liesel Tilles, P.O. Box 173, El Cerrito, CA 94530
(415) 524-5948

San Francisco/South Bay HELP
P.O. Box 4225, Mountain View, CA 94040
(408) 263-6360

Whittier HELP
Dawn Johnson
P.O. Box 4323, Whittier, CA 90607
(213) 944-6564

CONNECTICUT

Greater Hartford HELP
P.O. Box 456, New Britain, CT 06051

DISTRICT OF COLUMBIA

HELP of Washington
P.O. Box 32326, Washington, DC 20007 (mailing address)
1120 19th St., N.W., Washington, DC 20036
(202) 452-8408

FLORIDA

Palm Beach
Michael Raiman
228 N.E. 13th St., Del Ray Beach, FL 33444
(305) 272-6873

GEORGIA

Atlanta
ASHA/D. Smith
P.O. Box 76893, Atlanta, GA 30328
(404) 447-5414

ILLINOIS

Chicago HELP
P.O. Box 10112, Chicago, IL 60610

LOUISIANA

New Orleans
Harris Segal
1235 Carrolton Ave., Metarie, LA 70005

MARYLAND

Baltimore HELP
c/o Bill Palm, 111 N. Calvert St., Baltimore, MD 21202
(301) 396-4448

MASSACHUSETTS

Boston HELP
P.O. Box 1027 Back Bay Annex
Boston, MA 02117

MINNESOTA

Twin Cities HELP (Minneapolis/St. Paul)
c/o Marie Wilder, P.O. Box 3663, Minneapolis, MN 55403

NEW YORK

Long Island HELP
Mike Herships, P.O. Box 94 Port Jefferson, NY 11777
(516) 689-9483

New York HELP
70 W. 40th St., 4th Floor, New York, NY 10018
(212) 397-0938

OHIO

Cincinnati HELP
P.O. Box 19007, Cincinnati, OH 45219

Columbus HELP
P.O. Box 09441, Columbus, OH 43209

Toledo HELP
P.O. Box 6547, Toledo, OH 43612

OREGON

Portland HELP
P.O. Box 14934, Portland, OR 97214

PENNSYLVANIA

Philadelphia HELP
P.O. Box 13193, Philadelphia, PA 19101
Fran (215) 649-1349 (evenings)
Bill (215) 787-8294 (8 a.m.-4 p.m.)

Pittsburgh HELP
P.O. Box 6965, Pittsburgh, PA 15214

TEXAS

Dallas HELP
P.O. Box 38184, Dallas, TX 75238
(214) 742-9888 (M/W/F, 7 p.m.-11 p.m.)

Houston HELP
12870 Westhorpe, Houston, TX 77077
(713) 482-1987

WASHINGTON

Olympia HELP
c/o Health Services Sem., 2110, TESC, Olympia, WA 98505

Seattle HELP
P.O. Box 31171, Seattle, WA 98103

Tacoma HELP
P.O. Box 898, Tacoma, WA 98401

WISCONSIN

Milwaukee HELP
c/o Sixteenth Street Community Health Center
1036 South 16th Street, Milwaukee, WI 53204

The National Institute of Allergy and Infectious Diseases (NIAID), a unit of the National Institutes of Health (NIH), has produced a 28-minute film, **Jennifer**, that is now available to the general public.

The film is available for short-term free loan by writing to:
Modern Talking Pictures
Scheduling Department
5000 Park Street North
St. Petersburg, Florida 33709
(813) 541-6661

INDEX

ABOUT THE AUTHOR

Margaret O. Hyde is the author of an outstanding list of science books for young readers. The winner of a Thomas Alva Edison Award for "The Best Children's Science Book," she received her masters degree from Columbia University and received an honorary doctor of letters degree from Beaver College, her alma mater. Her latest books for McGraw-Hill include: MIND DRUGS, Fourth Edition, ENERGY: The New Look and MY FRIEND HAS FOUR PARENTS. Mrs. Hyde lives in Burlington, Vermont with her husband.